⌒OWNERSHIP

It's yours, God. It's not mine.

Leaders are stewards
of God's purposes
and resources in
human lives and
history. Too easily
we act as if we were
the owners. Too
easily we try to play
God. We do not
work miracles for
God. He does them
for us.

*Do not be afraid! . . . For the
battle is not yours, but God's.*
2 Chronicles 20:15

THIS is my one incessant prayer to you, hour by hour, day upon day: It's yours. I am not fighting this battle for you, God. It's your battle, and you are fighting for me. It is all yours, and I want whatever you have for me in this situation.

It is not my organization, it is yours, so I depend on your Spirit to show me what to do. These are not my people. I chose them and organized their efforts, but they do not belong to me. You entrusted them to my leadership, and they agreed to follow me. They deserve more and sometimes expect more of me than I can give them. What they really need is enormous. If I take their needs and hopes and fears on myself personally, I will be crushed instantly. They are yours.

So much depends on me, yet all I have for this task is whatever health and energy you give me—my eyes, ears, back, heart, lungs, knees, hands, feet, voice. I eat carefully, rest, exercise, and think positive thoughts, and still this wretched lump of clay fails me. You have creator's rights on my body. You formed every miraculous part. What you take away is your business. I will do what I can with whatever physical capability you give me. It's yours.

Yours is the kingdom, but we never seem to

have enough resources! We are always lacking something, our dreams always mocking our reality, our vision always dancing around our poverty. You own everything, so what we need must seem small to you. Show me where to look for it, how to know it when I see it, how to get it, how to use it best, and especially how to be content with it. It is all yours.

Time crawls relentlessly, mercilessly onward. The days end as the years end, with never enough time for all the good that could be done, only just enough for your priorities, if I get them right. You created time, and it does not limit you. But I do not have a thousand years today, God. I have only now.

I CHOOSE AND ORGANIZE PEOPLE, BUT THEY DO NOT BELONG TO ME.

So this day is yours; I am yours; these people are yours; the resources are yours. The challenges we face are yours, as is anything we hope to accomplish.

It's yours, God. It's not mine.

REFLECTIONS

A university colleague once explained what he thought was the key to the dramatic success we were witnessing. His view was that I had made the university *mine,* that I had taken personal responsibility for its destiny.

In one sense I understood his meaning and could agree with him. But the experience of freedom and creativity I enjoyed as president was possible precisely because the university belonged—humanly and legally—to the board of trustees and the church, not to me.

I had the privilege of proposing things, knowing that it was the board's job to stop me whenever they saw that I was about to dive into a pool with no water. I had the liberty to try things, knowing that if I failed, the board could choose to hire somebody else in my place. That freedom made me a better leader.

I could practice my stewardship of university leadership with a light, creative spirit because I did not have to bear the ultimate burden of ownership. It was not my job to make everything work out. Like leaders everywhere, my job was simply to follow the owner's desires and lead, helping to build great people by attempting something difficult and significant together.

In a spiritual sense, for both the trustees and me, every event, relationship, or decision ultimately belongs to God. Constantly practicing God's ownership liberates us for creative leadership. We just lead. All the rest is the Owner's business.

◡ REALITY

Show us what is real, God.
We have to know the truth.

Unless we are sure
of our starting
point, we can never
chart a correct
course to our goal.
There is no
alternative to the
freedom and power
of the truth.

Fix your thoughts on
what is true and honorable
and right.
Philippians 4:8

HELP us to agree on what is true about who we are and where we are, God, so that we may agree on where to go and the best way to get there. Though we will not all look at our reality in the same way, help us to see the same reality and agree on its meaning for us, whether or not we like what we see. Otherwise, God, we will waste precious time and energy arguing from different assumptions.

Obviously, you love variety! You made us so diverse that all we can do is laugh and wonder. That in itself is part of the reality we must understand. We each have our own reactions and feelings about everything. This wonderful range of perspectives helps us excel, as long as you help us to respect each other.

On my own it is not at all clear to me what is true, God. Often when I have felt the most certain, I have been deceived. So much in this world is merely a façade, not what it seems, and things change so fast that reality shifts like a moonlit shadow in the wind.

Somehow, God, in all our differences, and despite all the informational vagaries, give us a shared reality, a similar idea of how things truly are for us. Lead my spirit to the truth about our

RICHARD KRIEGBAUM

TYNDALE HOUSE PUBLISHERS, INC.
WHEATON, ILLINOIS

Edited by David Horton
Designed by Julie Chen

Library of Congress Cataloging-in-Publication Data

Kriegbaum, Richard.
   Leadership prayers / by Richard Kriegbaum.
     p.   cm.
   ISBN 0-8423-3689-3 (alk. paper)
   1. Leadership—Religious aspects—Christianity—Prayer-books and
devotions—English. I. Title.
BV4597.53.L43K75 1998
242'.88—dc21   98-19056

Printed in the United States of America

04 03 02 01 00
8   7   6   5   4

CONTENTS

Introduction	*vii*
Identity	1
Ownership	5
Reality	9
Wisdom	13
Values	17
Trust	21
Action	25
Delegation	29
Loss	33
Succession	37
Hope	41
Blessing	45
Fear	49
Weariness	53
Planning	57
Courage	61

Marketing	65
Failure	69
Communication	73
Strength	77
Budget	81
Integrity	85
Compassion	89
Anger	93
Board	97
Intuition	101
Creativity	105
Discouragement	109
Change	113
Love	117
About the Author	*121*

INTRODUCTION

Leadership Prayers is a book for those people who care enough about great leading and following to think rigorously about it and to open their spirits to do something about it. If you are now leading, want to lead, feel called to lead, are obliged to lead, or are responsible for choosing or guiding leaders, you will find this book valuable.

Leaders do not pray to inform God of what is happening. He already knows. And they do not pray to get him to do what they want. He already wants what is best for everyone involved.

Leaders pray to maintain the right relationship with God. From that relationship between the human spirit and the Spirit of God comes the divine perspective, insight, direction, and courage the leader must have to serve well. To keep from blundering into either hubris or despair requires a special sense of vision and balance that comes in a unique way from the Spirit of God through prayer. Ultimately, prayer determines the leader's effectiveness in what matters most—the eternal matters of the human spirit, including the leader's own spirit.

Jesus taught us to lead creatively and wisely, but he refused to tell us exactly how to do it. He just said that the Word of God must be our Truth, and that he would leave his Spirit to guide ours. He also told us to pray.

When we answer the call to lead, we commit ourselves to enable others to see their dream more clearly and somehow make it happen. That is spiritual business, and it cannot be done well without effective communication with the Spirit of God through prayer. When we lead well, exceptional achievement is possible. That is why we answer the call to lead. It is also why we follow great leaders. And it is why leaders pray so fervently.

By their nature, these prayers live only when they are internalized; they have power only when they are applied to real-life challenges. Skimming over them to get the main ideas will mean little because this is not a nifty new management technique. These are thoughts and prayers about leading people—not by the hand or by the nose or even by the intellect, but through the spirit.

Do not let the simplicity of these prayers fool you. If leadership were easy, everyone would be a great leader. Great leadership is from the spirit. The life of the spirit may be simple, even obvious, but it is never easy.

These are meant to be real prayers for individual leaders or for leadership groups, from the Board to an ad hoc task force. They evolved over many years of hard use while God was teaching me lessons I was not always sure I wanted to learn. They have been tested and confirmed by other leaders and have produced good results in me and the people I care about. I offer them to you as a pragmatic idealist trying to influence a chaotic and threatening world toward the values of the kingdom of God.

IDENTITY

It's not really me, God.
It's just what I do.

I lead as an expression of who I am, yet I must always be more than the leadership role I play. People may see me in terms of the visible leadership role which God has entrusted to me, but God knows who I really am. My integrity as a person—and as a leader—depends on seeing myself and what I do as God sees them.

Man looks at the outward appearance, but the Lord looks at the heart.
1 Samuel 16:7, NIV

GOD, this leadership role that I play from time to time, this character I assume, is a gift from you. You know I am not essentially the head of all this. I am merely your child, trying to become like you and do what you want.

Playing "leader" for a while is a great role in this real-life drama of The Good King vs. The Evil Prince. But unless you work a miracle, I will not play the role well, and the people I care about so much will suffer.

I know how the story goes: The Evil Prince tries to deceive, disrupt, and destroy anything good I might do. I know that in the long run truth wins, and at the very end good triumphs. I even know which ideas and values are supposed to control each character, including mine. But I also know that I have to write the script as I go and help other people play their parts. And I have to coordinate our script with all the other scripts in other parts of your kingdom. It is beyond me, but if you will whisper the cues, I will improvise.

Unless your Spirit informs and encourages me, I will not know how to play my part. I will stand foolishly silent on the stage, not knowing what I can do or even what I truly like to do. Worst of all, I will not know what I cannot do. Unless you intervene, I will blow my lines and miss my cues and confuse all the others. Help me sense my spiritual gifts so I will attempt only what you especially enable me to do and lead only where you are at work.

Do not let this leadership role consume me. Do not let me think that I have become my character. Remind my spirit who I really am so that when I go home I will not keep acting like the CEO. Guide me to do what is best for my family and for my own health.

Please help me keep it all straight. Leadership is extremely important, and I want intensely to do it right, but sometimes I forget where the role ends and I start. So I want your Spirit to remind me, however and whenever you have to . . .

It's not really me, God. It's just what I do.

3

IF YOU WILL
WHISPER THE
CUES, I WILL
IMPROVISE.

REFLECTIONS

The mother and daughter seated across the desk from me were very angry. Both felt that they had been misled about university housing and financial aid. The daughter seemed willing to state her case, hope for some concessions, and get back to her studies. But the mother contended with righteous intensity that it was the principle of the thing.

How could I, the president, allow such a thing to happen at a Christian university? It would be unacceptable even in a secular institution. She was mad, and she held me responsible.

I listened, acknowledged their pain and frustration, made sure they had appealed to the right staff people, apologized for any misunderstandings, asked what they specifically wanted me to do, and promised to look into it and get back to them.

My empathy for them was sincere, my inner spirit at peace. Why? Because I was able to separate my basic identity from my leadership role. I knew that these women did not hate me personally. They were simply enraged at whoever happened to be the president.

Whenever I base my identity or worth as a person on my role as a leader, I betray myself and miss God's best for me. I am not inherently the leader. I am God's child whom he dearly loves whether people are pleased or angry with my decisions, whether I succeed or fail.

My next appointment that day was with a couple who were thrilled with their child's experience at the university. I accepted their praise—but as the president, not personally. It works both ways.

situation, so that I can describe it in a way that leads us to consensus.

Some of us cannot see the truth because we fear it. Some of us invested heavily in another view of reality, and we may feel shamed if it turns out we were wrong. Some of us actually worked to build a different reality and do not want it to change.

I know that the truth tends to win in the long run, but I need to see it early enough to act wisely. Help us to understand our situation accurately so that we do not waste this opportunity for greatness. We want the truth because only the truth can free us to achieve our mission.

Show us what is real, God. We have to know the truth.

SOME OF US CANNOT SEE THE TRUTH BECAUSE WE FEAR IT.

REFLECTIONS

Standing under the brick arches and soaring columns of McDonald Hall, it was hard to remember that twelve years before I had sat cringing in a chapel service as I watched the rain drip from the roof directly onto our guest speaker.

It was my first year at a small college so poor that it couldn't even afford to repair its roofs, and I was charged with writing an institutional plan stating what it would take to survive. So many people had sacrificed so much for so long to keep the dream alive that my criticism seemed grossly unkind. But I believed that it was the truth of the situation and that we had to agree on our reality in order to focus our efforts.

We identified twelve barriers to our survival, agreeing that any one of them was potentially fatal if not reversed. I feared that complete demoralization would follow, key people would resign, donors would despair and then disappear, and I would attend a collegiate funeral.

Then an English professor named Wilfred Martens took me aside and said, "It really helps to look this all straight in the face and give it names and know what we have to do to succeed. We are not too tired. Now that we see it, I believe we can do this."

He was right. Twelve years later, Fresno Pacific was ranked fourth by *U.S. News & World Report* for overall best value among western regional universities.

⌒WISDOM

Teach me, God, so I have some wisdom to share.

If any of you lacks wisdom, he should ask God, who gives generously to all without finding fault, and it will be given to him.
James 1:5, NIV

There is no more precious gift for a leader than the wisdom that can apply relevant values to give meaning to our knowledge and experience.

WHATEVER you teach me is all I have for others, God. I must be wise if we are to succeed, and you know I am not naturally wise. Too often I am a fool, tricked so easily by my own personality, deceived by my ignorance, blinded by my proud determination to win, and misled by my logic. Sometimes my spirit is asleep or busy elsewhere or just encrusted with all my own exquisite rationalizing. I need your wisdom.

If I were brilliant, if I had the knowledge and strengths that I admire in so many other people, if I were a spiritual giant, I would simply ask you to help me do my best. But my best is not good enough. I do not know enough, and I cannot see clearly enough. I am your child, and I want to learn, but unless your Spirit teaches me, I have little to offer. I need your wisdom.

What you give me determines the success or failure of those I lead. They deserve some word, they need a message. How else will they understand our situation and how it informs our direction and points to a worthy purpose? I have studied and analyzed all I can. Teach me to go beyond the facts and feelings. My spirit waits quietly. I need your wisdom.

Teach me, God, so I have some wisdom to share.

I DO NOT KNOW
ENOUGH, AND
I CANNOT
SEE CLEARLY
ENOUGH.

REFLECTIONS

It happened again and again: the impasse, dialogue in circles, limited information and reasoning. In my early years, I thought all I needed was the best available information and some clear logic to get the best decision. Every good leader I have ever worked with wanted logic and information for important decisions.

But as I watched leaders who were consistently effective, I began to notice something else. Leading well eventually required more than the available information—something that gave it practical meaning. The best leaders could sense when that point had been reached. Instead of expecting to always have the final answer themselves, or otherwise forcing the issue to closure, they almost always paused—a moment behind closed eyes, a call for prayer, a break in the meeting, a bit of humor, seeking words from someone who had been silent. The list of methods was endless.

These leaders did not seem burdened or concerned when they exhausted knowledge and reason. The ragged edge that scared others seemed actually to assure them and guide them to wisdom. The best leaders knew after pausing who the wise person was for that moment— themselves or someone else. Such wisdom is a gift of the Spirit, and it is not lavished on leaders to cover their incompetence or indolence. This wisdom is the gracious contribution of God to those who truly lead in order to serve. It is an answer to sincere prayer.

⌒VALUES

*Infuse the right values in our
hearts, God. Start with me.*

Values control
behavior. We act
on the basis of what
we believe really
matters, what is
right and good.
Whoever influences
the core values in a
group is, in fact, the
leader. That process
must begin with the
values God instills
in the leader.

*Create in me a clean heart,
O God. Renew a right spirit
within me.*
Psalm 51:10

I REALIZE I cannot control everything, God, even through endless rules, regulations, and directives. I do not want an immobilized democracy in which everyone votes on every little thing. Nor do I want a demoralized dictatorship where I have to decide everything and think up everything. I want a true community with strong relationships and effective actions guided by commitment to the same core values.

We want the right values, those that make us a healthy community in which achieving our goals is our means of becoming better people and a better organization. So these values must move us toward the right goals. Guide our selection of these values. If we blunder here, nothing else will work right.

Your call to leadership always includes your provision of what I need to lead. By your grace I can do a lot of things to keep the right values before us and to model them myself, but only your Spirit can plant them deep and strong in everyone's heart. Make me a true spiritual leader, a nexus in the dynamic relationship of your Spirit and the spirit of these people I love.

I know the odds are against this working. It feels safer to try to tell everyone what to do instead of trusting them to act on their own in concert with these values. But help me to respect them as the individuals you created them to be so they can grow and be truly great for your glory.

I want to be a spiritually sensitive leader, to enable people to sense more clearly and powerfully the call and guidance of your Spirit in their lives. I know this kind of leadership is rare because it is a matter of the spirit, but, God, that is the kind of leader I want to be.

As the leader, I am responsible for the values we all live by. It must begin within me. Give me a healthy and strong spirit, for there is no going back. I feel a deep longing for the future. Help us to live the values that will take us there. I want it, God; I ache for it—for how things *could* be.

Infuse the right values in our hearts, God.

Start with me.

OUR VALUES MUST MOVE US TOWARD THE RIGHT GOALS.

REFLECTIONS

They had a truly noble mission, an inspiring vision, and a leadership disaster. The CEO was strong and convincing. He had rescued the place single-handedly, but unfortunately he was trying to run it the same way.

Masterful at sales, he was terrible at marketing. On the road he could present the concepts and programs of the organization, close the sale, and keep the revenue coming. But back home the staff doubted that he was representing them accurately. They did not trust him or follow him; they simply obeyed him. He could not watch and control all of them all the time, so each department did whatever seemed best.

The staff was competent and dedicated but plagued by confusion about the core values. Informal leaders were determining the operative values, which were increasingly at odds with what the CEO said and did. The resulting contradictions and inefficiencies threatened to overwhelm all their good intentions.

An effective leader will infuse the right mixture of values in an organization, like a tea bag infuses a cup of hot water. When this is done properly, the corporate culture absorbs the values so pervasively that it is no longer a cup of hot water; it is a unique cup of tea. Every part of the organization shares the same values; every drop tastes the same. Everyone knows what really matters, and they know that the leader lives with a passion for the same values as everyone else.

TRUST

*I know you love me,
and I trust you.*

The impossible
thought, the
transcending
miracle, is that the
awesome Creator
God of the universe
is my Father,
whom I can trust
completely as I do
my best to lead.

*We know and rely on
the love God has for us.
God is love.*
1 John 4:16, NIV

I LOVE you, God. You know I do. How natural it is to love you. You are perfect. You are beautiful, pure, powerful, absolutely truthful, and kind. You have been so generous to me that just saying thank you seems pitiful sometimes.

But far more powerful in my life is knowing and feeling that you love me. You know exactly and completely who I am—all my ugly thoughts, my mangled motivations, my pretending, my irrational fears, my pride, and my unfaithfulness—and you still love me. I know you love me.

You know me, and yet, because you love me, you let me lead others. I do not understand it, but I am grateful.

Because you love me, you want me to know the right thing to do, the right direction, the true meaning of every situation. You want me to choose wisely. You want what is best for everyone. You want me to see what you are doing, to understand the reality of things as you do.

I need a special gift of foresight, Father. I know your guidance is subtle; you are gentle with me. You do not shout orders, so I will wait for your Spirit to whisper what is true, shed light on what is wise, make sense of all the indicators. The choices may be mine, but the foresight and wisdom must be yours. I want to know your mind.

Because you love me, you never show me the future or tell me how things will turn out. I would never handle such knowledge well. But because you love me, you always want me to know the deep truth, to know what is possible and what is good. You never trick me or leave me. I trust you to lead my spirit to know what is real.

If you did not love me, there would be no hope or meaning in anything—no reason to lead, no reason to live. Your love is life itself.

YOU WANT ME
TO GET IT RIGHT,
TO CHOOSE
WISELY. YOU
WANT WHAT
IS BEST.

Because you love me, it is safe for me to love you in return. Because you love me, I can hear your Spirit of truth and find the right way to go. Because you love me, I can lead.

I know you love me, and I trust you.

REFLECTIONS

Normally, prayer is mainly talking to God, either publicly or privately. God is the consummate listener, and usually we just want him to listen to us.

However, it is quite another thing to ask God to speak to me, personally and directly, and for me to be able to listen and understand him. Sometimes it is scary when I talk to God, but the prophet Isaiah was right: It is patently terrifying when God speaks to *me*.

To take the risk of trusting myself with the awesome Creator of all things, I need reassurance that he loves me. I don't know exactly why I need to begin every event of deep spiritual searching by reminding myself that God loves me and that I can trust him to guide me. That is just how it always happens. When I fail to do this, when I race past this prayer and blurt out my problems or questions, God is understanding about it, but I can never hear clearly what he is saying.

Seeking God's guidance begins with an intense awareness that I can safely trust his love for me. When I am reassured of his love, then I feel safe to trust the quiet yes or no that concludes the issue, the picture of how things could be or should be, the guiding words that hang in my memory, the insight that eventually brings meaning and leads me to want what is right. The more God enables me to want the right things, the more freedom I experience to trust myself and lead as a powerful expression of who I am.

ACTION

I am not sure what to do, God, but here I go. Please make it work out right.

Leaders live for the action. It is our strength and our fatal attraction. The predetermined outcome does not require leadership and thus does not entice. We exist for the adventure in which we see the mighty hand of God.

We know that all that happens to us is working for our good if we love God and are fitting into his plans.
Romans 8:28, TLB

WHEN I am following you, God, I feel a bit lost most of the time. But that makes sense. I am not leading you. You are leading me.

If I want complete certainty, I cannot expect to be led by your Spirit. I cannot know what will happen next, nor demand control. And I know that following you is the only way I can make a great and beautiful difference in the world.

I cannot control what happens outside, but by your grace I can increasingly know myself. Help me to master who I am and how I give meaning to actions and events around me. May my wealth, power, and wisdom enable others to achieve extraordinary success. I know I can give freely of myself because in the economy of the Spirit, you always replenish my jar of oil.

I know when I am listening to you because your Spirit encourages me, points to the truth, lets me decide, and holds me accountable. And somehow you always make it work out. You provide the necessary resources: wisdom, strength, time, helpers, money, skills, and all the unanticipated things that I never could have planned for anyway. More wonderfully, you redeem my mistakes. You weave beauty out of my broken, mixed-up threads, not for my reputation or ego, but for the common good. Help me, God. The people I lead feel even more uncertainty than I do. They trust me, but they know I sometimes blunder.

I have done all the analyzing, conferring, thinking, planning, double-checking, and praying that I have time for. There is never enough information, and there are always conflicting opinions and priorities. I cannot sort it all out, but this is what seems best.

Is there anything else you want to tell me?

FOLLOWING YOU IS THE ONLY WAY I CAN MAKE A GREAT AND BEAUTIFUL DIFFERENCE IN THE WORLD.

It is time to act. I hope this is right for everyone involved. Now it is all up to you.

I am not sure what to do, God, but here I go. Please make it all work out right.

REFLECTIONS

Those who followed Jesus in the flesh were just as confused and uncertain as we often feel. He answered questions with ambiguous illustrations and more questions. He was not who they had planned for him to be. He was much more. The finale was not what they had expected. It was much better. Their path meandered over rough ground through dark nights, and they were lost until daybreak disclosed where they had been. By then they were on their own, guided only by the relationship they had known and the truth they had come to believe. It was enough. They were ready to lead.

They made mistakes. All leaders do. Perfectionists do not lead. Imperfect, passionate, true believers lead. They remind us that we cannot sit here forever and that until we act, God has nothing to work with. Leaders live on the edge, always squinting forward, always inventing, always convincing, forever building confidence among those they lead, but with no way to be absolutely certain. For leaders, every time is the first time.

Later, when the fog has lifted, we will see where we all wandered, the dangers we missed, the miracles, the serendipity of God's grace. Leading through the Spirit means depending on God to make things work out. The certainty of seeing comes after the action of believing.

The fearful ask, "Are you certain this is going to work?"

The honest answer is, "No, but we need to move ahead anyway."

28

DELEGATION

I cannot do this alone, God.
Who are the leaders I
sincerely should follow?

The highest form
of delegating is to
lay the leadership
mantle on key
people for particular
goals and then
follow their lead.

God takes the Spirit that
is on the leader and puts
it on the followers.
Numbers 11:17,
author's paraphrase

I KNOW only so much, God, and I can do only so much. If this organization is limited to my abilities alone, we will fall short of our potential together and miss your vision for us.

Help me identify other leaders for this effort. Enable me to see what each one can do best, show me how to recruit them, and point me to the right responsibility for the right person.

When I delegate, please give me the courage to release control and follow.

Sometimes I feel that leading is mostly about following, about deciding who is the best person to follow in some particular area. I depend on you to sharpen my intuition and sensitivity so I will choose the right people and delegate well.

How ironic, God, that the longer and better I lead, the more I depend on the skills and expertise of others. Someone else is better than I am at every task that needs to be done. They lead me in their areas. I must trust our success to them, so I must trust you to guide my selection of them.

I need you to enable me to get the right person to take responsibility for the right goal. Whose life situation, spiritual gifts, natural talents, interests, and motivation are right? Who is my leader in this area, God?

Help me to be clear about the distant goals and about who needs to do what to reach those goals. When I do this well, the spirit of the one to whom I delegate will respond with zeal. My own spirit will rejoice, and I will follow that person with confidence.

By your grace, my leadership will either enhance or restrain the work of your Spirit in those who lead with me, making them more effective or less effective. Those I choose to follow will have a profound impact on the results

in the organization, and they will have a profound impact on me.

Point me toward them, and make them greater leaders than I am.

I cannot do this alone, God. Who are the leaders I should follow?

THE LONGER AND
BETTER I LEAD,
THE MORE I
DEPEND ON THE
SKILLS AND
EXPERTISE OF
OTHERS.

REFLECTIONS

I learned the essence of delegation from Bill
Pollard. Before his years of executive leadership
with ServiceMaster Corporation, he was vice
president of Wheaton College. One fall the direc-
tor of computer systems resigned suddenly just
as school was starting. By November no replace-
ment had been found, frustrations were rising
rapidly, and Bill called me in to propose that I take
the position. I was a Spanish teacher at the time.

I pleaded gross technical ignorance, but he
explained that we could solve the technical problems once we had solved the people and systems
problems. I figured if he was brave enough to offer
it to me, I would be brave enough to try it. I sus-
pect neither of us understood how little the other
one knew about computer systems.

He made it plain to me that the whole institution depended on the computer system, that users
were angry, and that it was my mess to clean up.
He offered suggestions, required progress reports,
and expected results, but he followed my lead and
he supported me, even to the point of releasing
staff and creating policy. I responded to his thor-
ough and masterful delegation by working, learning,
growing, and producing like never before.

Bill Pollard is a godly man and a powerful leader.
I doubt that he would ever say he was a follower
of Rich Kriegbaum on anything whatsoever. But
with me he was better than he knew. He dele-
gated—and developed my leadership from his
followership.

LOSS

Oh, God, heal these wounds.

Change often
wounds people,
and the leader who
champions those
changes has a
unique reason to
stay close to the
wounded.

I am the Lord who heals you.
Exodus 15:26

GOD, this organization is perpetually on the road to the future: relocating, reorganizing, revising, restructuring, retooling, reinventing. And all this change results in an endless string of bruises, dislocations, cuts, strains, and breaks. No matter how I do it, and no matter how necessary it is, every change hurts someone. Comfort me, Father, so your healing can flow to those I lead.

There is so much pain in this world, God. So much loss of health, energy, love, opportunity, happiness, security, and due reward. These wounds are very real. So many of us are working wounded every day; it is a miracle that we accomplish so much. Touch us, Father. Console us. Heal us. I know you love each of us, even those who choose to live far away from you or who injure themselves needlessly.

The loss we cannot control is bad enough, God, but how I hate it when we do it to ourselves. We try to function like a family, but when family members hurt each other, it is worse than if we did not care about each other at all. Our caring for each other binds us together, but the grief is all the more intense when feelings are hurt and relationships are severed. We need your healing.

We try to work like a body, and we all feel pain whenever one of us has a problem. It doesn't seem to matter what the problem is; the pain spreads to others. I feel for those who hurt, but for the good of everyone, we need to keep going. Heal us.

The separations never seem to stop. We work very hard to evaluate, select, and integrate people in the organization. Then when one of them has to leave us, it really hurts. Even if we believe you have truly called that person to some other service, we still mourn the loss of relationship.

Firing people is the worst of all, God. When I have to tell people that they don't fit the needs of the organization or we can't afford them, they feel betrayed. When they joined us, I told them how important they were, and now no matter how I say it, my message makes them feel unimportant—to us or to anyone else. Maybe not even important to you.

We are doing everything we can to cover these

WE ALL FEEL PAIN WHENEVER ONE OF US HAS A PROBLEM.

human losses, but beyond money and time and kind words, there is still the pain and grief that you must heal. Have mercy on all the hurts and fears among us, including the pain we have inflicted on ourselves.

Oh, God, heal these wounds.

REFLECTIONS

As a leader, I spend a lot of time at funerals of all kinds: the death of a physical body, the death of a marriage, the death of a friendship, the death of a career, the death of a department or a team, the death of a dream, a hope, a legend.

Though there is often little or nothing that I can actually do, I am needed at the point of human and organizational crisis. My caring creates my credibility.

At a graveside I stand in for everyone in the organization, leading through the silence and darkness with an embrace, a moment of direct eye contact, or just my presence. Somehow, in a mysterious process known only deep in our spirits, some of God's healing flows.

I sometimes witness the agony when people unwillingly meet the end of their service in the organization. Not really ready to retire, or perhaps being released, they suffer the wounds of separation as the corporate knife cuts the flesh of human bonds and feelings that are as real as they are intangible.

Every corporate change has a human price that is just as real as the price of personal illness, injury, and loss. Leading the changes in the organization puts me close to the pain. And if I helped bring the pain, the least I must do is be present to bless the healing with prayer.

⟨SUCCESSION

I will not last forever, God.
Where are my replacements?

Jesus called his twelve
disciples to him and gave
them authority.
Matthew 10:1

As soon as the vision
is announced, the
leader must begin
succession planning
and selection, just
as Jesus did.

HELP me remember, God, that I can be reassigned, neutralized, or eliminated for a thousand different reasons at any moment. My leadership is precarious, hanging by the silver thread of people's trust in me. Countless things over which I have no control can break that thread, including your call elsewhere, and I will be gone.

But they need a leader, and when I am gone they must have others to turn to, others whom they trust, who can tell them the truth. Show me those who can lead after me and better than me. Ruffle my spirit when they are near, quicken my heart when I feel their power, and open my eyes to see the special effect they have on people.

Protect me from preserving my own position or power or perspectives at the expense of future leaders. When they point out where I have not led well, shut my mouth and open my heart. Help me make it safe for them to try new things. Let me touch the spirit of those who possess the heart of a servant. I want to know them and love them and watch their energy flow into others around them. I want to claim them for this work and pray them into my place.

I will not have the privilege of choosing who will lead after me. Others will decide that. But I can help prepare leaders, and I can help the organization be ready for them.

Show me the ones who challenge me, the ones with more freedom and stronger faith than I have. Point out the ones who love people better than I do, who lead because they really care about people. Make the spiritual giants visible to me. Let me notice the ones who attract loyal, high-quality friends.

Help me distinguish between the confident and the arrogant, between the humble and the hesitant. Bring out the strong ones who can carry their own burdens and also the burdens of others. Allow tough times that will yield success to those who refuse to give up. Help me advance the leaders for the future.

Oh, God of mercy, don't let me stay in this job one day too long. And don't let this all fall apart after I leave.

I will not last forever, God. Where are my replacements?

I CAN HELP
PREPARE
LEADERS, AND
I CAN HELP THE
ORGANIZATION BE
READY FOR THEM.

REFLECTIONS

In June after my twelfth year at Fresno Pacific University, my wife, Elona, and I drove to the coast for our annual day of considering whether the fiscal year just starting should be my last in the role of president. That day, as always, I spent time on each element of the succession prayer. I asked myself whether what yet needed to be done still sent eager fire through my belly. I envisioned other leaders in my place. I relived my successes and faced the things I had gotten wrong or left undone. The institution was maturing beautifully, and I felt that my evolving leadership could meet the emerging needs. I pondered where we were, Elona and I, on the path of our own pilgrimage as individuals and as a couple.

By midday I had to admit that I had no peace about continuing. The years ahead looked wonderful, but I could no longer see myself as the president. We were both stunned to silence. In the weeks that followed, we began to see that God had completed what he had called us there to do, and in October I resigned. It was the single most difficult—and most important—decision of my tenure. Subsequent years confirmed that I had gotten it right. It was good for the university and good for me. Leadership succession plays out in the departure of the incumbent, and departing well depends on intentional prayer.

⌒HOPE

....

*You are the God of hope. Give me
something to hang on to.*

Even though we
have the promise
of a grand finale,
we need hope along
the way. As long as
we have hope, there
is a future. Because
leadership is for the
future, leaders are
hope dealers.

*Those who wait on the Lord
will find new strength.*
Isaiah 40:31

HOPELESSNESS will kill us, God. Normally our goals are what energize us, but not when we think they are impossible. Then they drag us down like death chains until we can cut them loose. We have to be honest with each other. We need reality, not fantasy, but we have to hope for something, and it has to be worth the effort.

If we lose all hope, we will never know whether we could have succeeded—and we will fail. I cannot tell these people to hope for something I do not believe is possible. Is it all over, or is there something I do not see? Is this the end, or is there another way to go? What have I missed? What are you up to?

I will let go of this hope if that is what I need to do, but I do not want to give up too soon. If you have a surprise of grace hidden somewhere, it sure feels like I need a hint of it now. Despairing people will not even be able to move far enough to stumble upon your solution. We are about to give up.

This is not a crisis of faith, God. We still believe in you. We trust you. This is a crisis of hope. We are about to slip into despair, and we need a basis for hope.

When we claimed this hope in faith, we knew

it was a very great challenge. That is why we needed great hope, and that great hope gave us great energy and determination. By faith I have been moving ahead, telling them it should work out, saying that we can make it.

I have been here before with you, God. I can walk on in faith forever, I guess, and others will trust and follow me—for a while. But eventually they must have some solid hope—something they can honestly accept themselves, some reason to keep going until we reach our goal.

I do not need hope when I can see the goal, but I cannot see anything right now, God. So all I have is hope.

You are the God of hope. Give me something to hang on to.

I CANNOT SEE THE GOAL RIGHT NOW, SO ALL I HAVE IS HOPE.

REFLECTIONS

When I joined Fresno Pacific University, many people had gotten used to annual deficits and figured that spending a little more would not make any significant difference. Once we finished a year in the black—barely—almost everyone realized that small things mattered. They worked hard to control expenditures as long as they thought there was some reasonable hope of finishing in the black again.

If the word got around that we were likely to have a deficit no matter what, many lost hope and tended to spend more freely. Their reasoning was determined by whether or not there was any realistic hope of reaching the goal. The values of the community were strong enough that as long as there was some hope, most people were willing to sacrifice for a shot at an important goal. They had doubts, but they still had hope.

There is risk in every leadership situation. If adversity and the risk of failure were not real, the satisfaction of success would not be real either. Because there is risk, some people will lose confidence—they will doubt. But people can accomplish great things despite having doubts.

Hope is different from confidence. The opposite of hope is despair. Very few people can sacrifice much if they have no hope. Balancing hope with reality is one of the basic arts of leadership. We seek to inspire confidence. If confidence is impossible, then at least hope. If not the *likelihood* of success, at least the *possibility*.

➣BLESSING

I need your blessing, Father.
Show me that I really
matter to you.

Does God really
care about our
efforts? The leader
seeks to influence
the organization
to significant
achievement, but
above all the leader
seeks assurance of
God's blessing, with
or without other
measures of success.

The Lord's blessing is our
greatest wealth.
Proverbs 10:22, TLB

THE BEST I can offer you, God, is the excellence of my work—my sincere worship. But you are perfect, and my best is still shabby next to your work. I do not deserve your favor, God. I cannot earn your blessing on my work, my life, or this organization, no matter how good I am. Still, my heart longs to present love gifts you will cherish, and I desire your blessing.

What I am doing seems important to many, but human praise can fool me. Oh, God, do not abandon me to live on human blessing alone and miss your blessing. Help me to know the difference between success and blessing.

What matters to me is whether I really matter to you. Is this the most important thing I am supposed to be doing? Am I moving in the right direction? Am I doing it in a way that pleases you? My work adds nothing to your blessing, but your blessing means everything to my work.

I know that not all your blessings are pleasant. If I am not leading this organization on the right course, then bless me with a sign of redirection, no matter how tough that blessing has to be. I will accept it as your true and loving favor poured out on me and those I lead.

Make me a means of your grace to the
people I lead—a blessing from you to them.
Do not let anything about me or what I do disrupt the flow of your blessing to them. Do not
let me prevent your blessing on this organization
by being or doing anything that dishonors your
name.

Let me know your special favor, whether in
your pleasant blessings or in the unpleasant ones.
No matter what I may think of myself or what
others may say . . .

Show me that I really do matter to you.
I need your blessing, Father.

HELP ME TO
KNOW THE
DIFFERENCE
BETWEEN
SUCCESS AND
BLESSING.

REFLECTIONS

A pastor friend told how, when he was a boy, a particular uncle would sometimes place his giant hand on the boy's head and lovingly rough up his hair. It was a silent blessing that was so cherished that my friend remembers sliding near in hopes of the special attention. The man's touch told the boy that he was noticed and that he mattered. A lifetime later, the blessing still worked its affirming ministry.

On homecoming weekend I attended a reunion luncheon of the alumni who had graduated in the very first years of the school's half century of operation. I listened to reminiscences and said a few presidential words.

The next week the organizer visited my office. Her gratitude was simply stated. "Thank you for blessing us. You made us feel like we still matter."

We all search for meaning in life, the sense of God's pleasure in who we are and what we do, the shimmer of God's blessing. In organizations or movements it can come in divers ways, but always it must be able to come through the leader. Whether in a committee or a nation, wise followers must choose leaders through whom God can bless them.

The heavenly Father touched his Son and told the world, "You are my beloved Son, and I am fully pleased with you" (Luke 3:22). Even the Son of God needed blessing. Without it, nothing else matters. With it, no miracle is impossible.

FEAR

I'm afraid you won't do what I expected, God. Give me your peace.

Once in a while the leader's fear is pure panic or demoralizing dread. But for most leaders most of the time, fear is not immobilizing terror; it is nagging anxiety, wondering if things will work out the way it seems they should. It is basically fear of failure.

Don't be afraid, for I am with you. Do not be dismayed, for I am your God.
Isaiah 41:10

I'VE TOLD you many times what my heart longs for, God. I want all our research and planning, our hopes and dreams, our extra work and sacrifices, our prayers, and our sincere motives to produce a great result. I want us to succeed.

I want us to reach the goal we set; I want us to exceed it! I want all these people to share the roaring ecstasy of success. I want them to gain confidence and believe in themselves and in the way we went about it.

Most of all, I want them to believe in you. I want people to say, "Wow! That is amazing. Look what God did there!" I want people to praise you for this accomplishment because they know that I am trying to do what you want.

But I wonder if you are going to do it.

I talked with you about this all along the way, and I did my best to understand what you wanted us to do. Still, I worry that you might do something else, something unexpected. You know that I do not want anything less than your best for me and for the organization. But what will happen if this fails?

Maybe you have lessons you need to teach me through failure. Maybe the process is more important than the outcome. Maybe this is just a small part of something much bigger that is not yet apparent. Maybe success will lead to problems I cannot foresee.

I do not fear the odds or the competition; I trust your power. I am not afraid you will hurt me; I trust your goodness and wisdom. I am more afraid of embarrassment. I am afraid of failing. That will make me feel stupid, God, and others will doubt me.

If this fails, maybe I need to step aside. Maybe you are signaling that we need somebody else to lead. Do not let this fail because of me. Get me out of the way if you have to, God, but let these people know success.

You are my God, this is your work, and I know you care about our success or failure. I will give you my fear if you will give me your peace. I admit . . .

I WANT YOUR BEST FOR ME AND THIS ORGANIZATION. BUT WHAT IF THIS FAILS?

I'm afraid you won't do what I expect, God. Give me your peace.

REFLECTIONS

The beginning of leadership wisdom is the fear of the Lord, the acknowledgment that although we can never control or even predict what God does, we must lead anyway.

Jesus told his disciples to get into a boat and row through the night to the other side of the great lake. They did exactly as he instructed and almost immediately were hit by such a windstorm that they were essentially stalled.

Exhausted in the middle of their all-night catastrophe, the disciples were scared witless when Jesus suddenly appeared, walking toward them like a ghost on the water. Peter nearly drowned when Jesus invited him, too, to walk on the water. After all the trouble, Jesus calmed the very storm that had prevented the disciples from doing what he had told them to do!

When God gives us a goal, we naturally expect him to help us succeed, not send a storm to block us. We row like mad all night, trying to get to the goal on the distant shore, little contemplating that God might meet us on the way.

Following God is not always a neat and tidy achievement. It is often a humbling—even fearful—confrontation of the unexpected and the uncontrolled. Leadership has to do with trusting God's great purposes in the lives of those who act. The ones who slept on the shore that night missed the whole adventure!

WEARINESS

I'm worn out, God.
My spirit is weary.
I need your
renewing strength.

He gives power to those who
are tired and worn out; he
offers strength to the weak.
Isaiah 40:29

God's call always
comes with God's
empowerment,
but our human
limits are real, and
the weariness of
leadership must be
respected in honest
humility.

WHEN I first felt the call of leadership taking hold of my heart, God, I began feeling your special strength coming into me also. The leader's burden is very strong in me, but so is the corresponding gift of your divine empowerment. That power has always confirmed my call and reinforced my confidence to lead.

I am amazed—and so is everyone else at times—at what I can do and at how light this burden feels. It fits me with perfect comfort, and I love it and thank you for it. Sometimes it feels like nothing is impossible as you strengthen me for this role.

But despite the energizing vision and the power of your Spirit, I am weary. I tried to do more than my body or mind could accomplish. I did not maintain healthy boundaries for myself and said yes to more than I could do excellently. Settling for average drains my strength, God.

I acted as though I could not trust you to bring the success I longed and prayed for. I acted as though I had to do it all myself. I wanted it whether you did or not. In the process I disrespected you, presuming to take your place.

With hubris I worked as though I had no normal human limits. I am sorry for it, Father. I am feeling very human now, and my limits are more clear. I ask your Spirit to guide me back to my proper boundaries, not for my ease or comfort, but so I can lead in humble faith.

You promised me the strength I would need for this leadership, and I did not believe you. I tried to go beyond the strength you gave, and I have exhausted myself. What a faithless fool!

I am weary of the adversity, weary of the relentless expectations, and weary of not having a life of my own outside the organization. I am weary of explaining things over and over and weary of acting cheery and positive when I feel tired and confused.

It was not always this way. Once the effort felt joyous, even exhilarating. I think it can be that way again if I can learn from your Spirit how to walk humbly with you rather than proudly ahead of you.

I TRIED TO GO
BEYOND THE
STRENGTH YOU
GAVE, AND I HAVE
EXHAUSTED
MYSELF.

Please give me all the strength I need to lead well, and I will be content with that. I will not try to force the results I want. I confess . . .

I'm worn out, God. My spirit is weary. I need your renewing strength.

REFLECTIONS

My typical weekday pattern is to rise early and do my morning routine: matinal prayers, a shave, a physical workout, and a shower before a breakfast of fruit. Then I put on my CEO or consultant costume—including a tie.

Sometimes toward evening I loosen my tie, but I have learned to pull it up before leaving my office. While some people look casual and confident with a loosened tie, it just makes me look tired and frazzled. Even the appearance of weariness in the leader creates a weary organization.

Real weariness comes not from working long and hard but from attempting something for which I am not well suited or trying more than God made me capable of doing. I may blunder into weariness from my insecurity or work addiction or some other compulsion. Regardless of the cause, every time I force my outcome instead of allowing God to do his will, someone pays the price.

Better that God should allow me to "hit the wall" than to let others suffer for my excesses. When it happens, I must not blame others or give up. I must learn anew to walk by faith within the limits of my true self and God's true call. I will always be testing those limits, but I must always be ready to humbly admit my weariness and seek God's renewal or redirection.

⌘PLANNING

*God of our future, show me your
way. Make our plans wise.*

*"For I know the plans I
have for you," says the Lord,
"They are plans for good
and not for disaster, to give
you a future and a hope."*
Jeremiah 29:11

God has plans to
prosper his people.
His human leaders,
serving under his
call, also make
plans, seeking to
bring the affairs
of this world into
closer conformity
with God's eternal
and perfect plan.

SHOW me your way for us, God. In all the data, there are patterns I must see. Among the many indicators, there are wise directions I must choose. By your grace I must peer through the foggy confusion and glimpse the light glimmering far ahead. Help me to choose the right path and head toward the right marker. If I am wrong, we could be obliterated. Guide me.

Wisdom alone will not automatically make our plans easy to adopt or implement. Inevitably, wise planning will require us to act before it is completely apparent that we need to do so. For most of us, that will be hard to do, and it will be frightening for some. The comfort and security of the present that we worked so hard to create will try to seduce us. Nostalgia for our past will tempt us to stay there. Help me instill a longing for our future the way you see it. Carry us forward, God.

Help us to let go of the present we worked so hard for, the present we asked you for, so that we may embrace a new and better future. Prepare us to accept some chaos in the short run in order to make things better in the long run, to take resources that could feed our present strengths and current welfare and risk them on an uncertain future.

As the leader, I speak for the future, and I love planning to get there. But this is very painful and threatening for some. Help me use the planning process to bring them along. Give me planning wisdom, God.

Help us to move fast enough to reach our best future in time for it to matter. But let us move wisely enough that we can all stay together. Our inheritance lies yet ahead. Oh, God, help us claim it. I am looking for your guiding light.

God of our future, show me your way. Make our plans wise.

HELP US TO LET
GO OF THE
PRESENT SO THAT
WE MAY EMBRACE
A BETTER
FUTURE.

REFLECTIONS

The president pointed to a large box on his credenza. "We need an institutional plan," he explained. "I have been collecting the stuff in that box for over a year. Our plan is in that box. I want you to find it and write it down for us. I will be praying for you." He was absolutely serious.

I spent the whole summer in my basement with that box—plus a lot of additional material—creating the initial discussion draft of a comprehensive plan to advance the organization. The president was a strong spiritual leader, but he had no heart for the drudgery of planning. When I brought in the draft, he thanked me and confirmed that he had indeed been praying for me.

In countless settings I have asked participants to describe the kind of leader they would personally follow. Not once has anyone ever said that the ideal leader should be a great planner. What they do always identify is vision, the enhanced ability to describe the present situation and the desired future in a way that inspires action. I do not fault my presidential friend for asking me to draft his plan. He sensed that a plan was needed, and he made sure one was developed. In time the vision was refined, and with his support it became a wonderful reality. I am convinced that his prayer truly enabled the planning process to create a compelling vision that became a new corporate reality.

COURAGE

Thank you for the wisdom, Lord.
Now give me the courage to act.

Unlike managers, leaders accept unlimited liability for the overall good of the organization. In doing so, leaders also accept responsibility for certain decisions that require not only wisdom but courage.

Act with courage, and may the Lord be with those who do well.
2 Chronicles 19:11, NIV

WISDOM first, Lord! I feel like I am tiptoe-ing between wisdom and folly. I am either a genius or an idiot. I am so action oriented that I had plenty of courage to charge off before the whole picture was complete. Things looked simpler and easier. Courage is tougher now that I see everything more fully. I really need courage now, Lord.

It seems wise to move ahead, but I know there will be a price to pay. Good people whom I respect feel strongly that we should go another direction. They may be angry or hurt if I proceed. I may lose some dear friends and major support for our organization and for our mission—maybe forever. Is it really worth it, God?

Why does it have to be so hard when we are all trying to do what is right? I really did my best to actively listen to the concerns of others and to carefully explain this thing to everyone. Still, here we are. If this truly is the right thing to do, why does it look like it is going to hurt the organization? Is this difficult because I am wrong, or despite my being right? Doing the right thing—morally and prac-tically—should make me feel blessed. Why doesn't it?

This isn't just about me, Lord. Every day at every level of the organization, people make decisions with moral or ethical implications. Help them to know what is right in your sight, and give each one the courage to do it, every time.

In the long run, we should prosper by this course of action. But there is no long run if we do not survive the short run. I will trust that this particular short run will not destroy us. And if it does, I will trust you to take us through that also.

Thank you for the wisdom, Lord. Now give me the courage to act.

IT SEEMS WISE
TO MOVE AHEAD,
BUT I KNOW
THERE WILL BE
A PRICE TO PAY.

REFLECTIONS

Several weeks before I was to start as vice president of Fresno Pacific, the financial officer called to explain that the administrative computer system was in total collapse. I arrived in July. By October we had evaluated our options and prepared a recommendation for the church convention and the meeting of trustees. We found a computer, a software system, and a maintenance contract for a quarter of a million dollars.

The problem was that the institution had accumulated an operating deficit in the same amount. My first public action as a new administrator would be to ask a small church conference to approve doubling the debt of a struggling college that some thought should be shut down.

Courage is not an absolute virtue. A brave fool cannot lead any better than a fearful sage can. We believed we had as wise a plan as time and conditions allowed, but we needed the courage to propose yet more debt to skeptical owners. We knew there were powerful people who would oppose us. The decision could break the college if it failed.

Courage is contagious, just like fear. When champions stood up, the audacious proposal gained support and was approved. By January we were digging out, and in June an unexpected gift more than balanced the budget.

God honors the courage prayer if it follows the wisdom prayer.

MARKETING

Our image is all we have in the market, Lord. Keep us honest, and protect us.

The success of the organization depends on having enough people in the market exchange with us. Their decisions are determined by their perceptions of whether we offer the best available solution to their felt needs. They decide based on image. In terms of marketing, image is everything.

Choose a good reputation over great riches.
Proverbs 22:1

IT IS so frustrating, God! We work so hard, but being the best—or offering the best value—does not guarantee our success. We do all we can to be honest and creative in all our marketing messages, but that does not guarantee success either.

It is hard to succeed in this media-defined environment, where image is reality. The market acts only on its perceptions—not on how good we really are, only on how good it thinks we are. The lie can be big and brazen or small and subtle, but the lie often lasts long enough to beat the truth. Honor the truth, Lord.

The truth tends to win in the long run, I know, but too often there is no long run. Conditions don't always last long enough for the truth to prevail. We are determined to market ourselves as skillfully as we possibly can, but, Lord, keep us honest. Don't let us slip into exaggerating or misleading in any way. Give us a passion for making the truth convincing.

I don't want to whine to you if we are losing fairly in the marketplace. But, Lord, if we do it right and tell the truth, then we are depending on you to protect our reputation and our place in the market from those who would destroy us unfairly. I ask you to let our image match reality.

Don't let me mistake my own petty prejudices for the truth of what people really need, or mistake people's felt needs for their real needs. Help me to know what people really need so I can serve them well.

Keep us true to your values, Lord, whether we seem to be succeeding or not. If you allow an undeserved image to be decisive, I will still do my best to honor you in everything we do as an organization. I would rather fail than dishonor your name.

Our good name matters only if it is under your great name. Lord, by your providence may we have the image in the market of being the best at what we are trying to do, and by your grace may that image be accurate.

Our image is all we have in the market, Lord. Keep us honest, and protect us.

KEEP US TRUE TO YOUR VALUES, LORD, WHETHER WE SEEM TO BE SUCCEEDING OR NOT.

REFLECTIONS

No one has ever provided a better example of marketing than Jesus did. He inherited a situation in which his movement, the kingdom of God on earth, had been taken over by small-minded legalists who had reduced its majestic principles to a rigid set of codified behaviors. Its inspiring orientation toward the future had become a stultifying preoccupation with history and tradition. Its singular focus on right relationships with people and with God had been refracted into an array of social castes. Its image ranged from necessary nuisance to irrelevance.

In three years Jesus "repositioned" the kingdom of God so thoroughly in so many people's minds that when he physically departed, the movement raced on, expanding and maturing in its new form and direction. He accomplished this feat not through selling, advertising, or promotion but by investing heavily in strong personal relationships with a small group of dedicated persons whose thinking he profoundly reshaped. He consistently modeled the values of the kingdom, and he described its true nature. Above all, he always started with people at the point of their felt needs— their wants, fears, and hopes. Then he skillfully guided them to discover their real needs and see their potential.

The compelling new image of the kingdom attracted a vast new public. There were detractors, false advertisers, cheap imitations, and lower-priced alternatives, but the kingdom prevailed. That is perfect marketing.

⟨FAILURE

Oh, God, I really messed up this time. How will you get me out of this one?

The leader
serves the God
of redemption,
who buys back our
blunders and sins
and weaves them
[He] redeems your life   into the fabric of
from the pit.   a beautiful future.
Psalm 103:4, NIV

YOU ARE the God of redemption. That is a good thing because I feel like I am the servant of disasters. I feel like I make more mistakes in an average week than most people do in a year, and you watch me do it. Of course you watch me take more risks, too. I don't know any other way to lead.

Still, I hate it when it is my own fault that things go bad. You know how I bring you the disasters that other people create. I gladly let you own them. But this is my own failure. I am so sorry about it that I wish I could hide it and try to take care of it myself. I can't, and I know it would be stupid to try.

So here I am again. I did this one myself, it is big, and anything I do will probably just make things worse. I need your redemption of this whole event.

If I had listened better—with both heart and head—maybe this would not have happened. Use this to help me trust you more completely, follow you more closely, bring my stuff to you automatically. I need to learn from this fiasco. Show me how I can be part of your solution instead of part of my problem.

Thank you for trusting me with the lessons I must learn from this, but please spare the people I lead. I have really let everyone down by my failure. It is not their fault, God; it's mine. I never want to embarrass the followers who have trusted me.

The truth is I am a fallen leader right now with weakened credibility. Whether I can get up from this and still lead, or even serve in any other way, is up to you. I am glad this mess is yours because you always know how to make things work out for my good. What a miracle is your redemption!

I commit myself to be the best steward I can be of whatever new challenges your solution will create for me or the organization. And I commit myself to admit my failure to the organization and accept responsibility for it. You know how expert I am at rationalizing and blaming. Don't let me

I COMMIT MYSELF TO ADMIT MY FAILURE AND ACCEPT RESPONSIBILITY FOR IT.

do that. Whatever forgiveness you put in their hearts is your business. My business is to honestly own my personal failure and look for your redemption.

Oh, God, I really messed up this time. How will you get me out of this one?

REFLECTIONS

Within six weeks I knew in my gut I had made a dreadful error. I had enthusiastically endorsed the hiring of a grossly incompetent staff member. He had one great attribute, however: unwavering determination. He fought us every grudging step. We lost a small fortune, wasted three years, and damaged our reputation before I could finally get him out.

Learning from failure is the hard work of leadership. Learning from success is much more fun. But if I am leaning forward, if I am taking the risks of visionary leadership, sometimes I will fail. Worst of all, sometimes those failures will not be just technical or planning failures; they may be failures of the spirit, failures of moral or ethical character, or even failures of sheer folly—like not waiting to check one more reference.

It was not easy to admit that I was guilty of such a highly visible and costly failure, and it was no consolation that everyone else had been fooled too. I admitted my failure to the staff, explained what I had learned from it, and requested forgiveness and support to keep leading. My action set an important example. I made it plain that leaders must take reasonable risks and, in the process of leading, will sometimes fail. When they do, they must own it openly but not let it crush them.

If I fail too often or make a fatal mistake, I shouldn't be leading. But if I *never* fail, I am not really leading.

COMMUNICATION

*Let me listen to the words of
their spirits. And let me speak
words from your Spirit.*

The more change
an organization
experiences,
the more it
needs effective
communication,
especially to and
from the leader.

*May the words of my mouth
and the thoughts of my heart
be pleasing to you, O Lord,
my rock and my redeemer.*
Psalm 19:14

I T SEEMS like nothing happens silently among us, God; everything requires words. There are so many words for every event, every dream, every meeting, every relationship, every plan, and especially every change. In fact, my leading seems to be mostly words: the words that I hear or read and the words that I speak or write.

I want the organization to change in order to change the world, but mostly what changes is our words. To do things differently, we need different ideas, and the ideas need just the right words. What power the right words have, God! They bring our inner reality to life and make our external reality comprehensible for us.

Good words clarify, strengthen, and encourage us. The wrong words confuse us and leave us weakened and discouraged. Oh, Lord, give each of us the good words and the good listening we need to be a great organization.

You are such a listener, God! Help me listen to your Spirit so I will be able to listen to the unspoken messages people bring to me. I want to listen the way you do.

Make me genuinely accessible. People come with their words, but they hope I will hear their hearts. Whether they speak or write, teach me how to be truly quiet inside and actively listen. I do not want to disrespect them by interrupting or pretending to listen while I secretly ignore them so I can think about what I am going to say. I want to really listen and understand their hearts. Help me open my mind and heart, not just my office door. I cannot lead well if I cannot listen well.

I need your messages, for the organization and for those outside. If I speak and write accurately and convincingly, people's ideas will change and the organization will advance. If I speak unclearly or weakly, it will all get worse. My silence is better than wrong words, so guide me, Lord. Help me to hear and to speak the truth in love.

I want my words for others to be your words for me. I know that you do most of your teaching and nurturing in my life when you are preparing me to present ideas to others. I need your Spirit to shape my thoughts so that when I express who I am as a leader, I will be your servant doing your work with your words. Speak to me, and speak through me.

75

PEOPLE COME WITH THEIR WORDS, BUT THEY HOPE I WILL HEAR THEIR HEARTS.

Let me listen to the words of their spirits. And let me speak words from your Spirit.

REFLECTIONS

When I ask search committees or leadership semi-
nars what they want in a leader whom they personally would follow, they invariably want a convincing
communicator and often forget that they also want
to be heard and respected. Communication is such
a dominant factor in leadership success that it is
easy to mistake a great communicator for a great
leader.

Like most people, I entered leadership partly on
the strength of my ability to use words to influence
people to do things they would not otherwise
attempt. It took many years to learn the dance of
collaborative leadership in which one partner leads
and the other follows with a carefully rehearsed
and trusting mutuality that allows enormous freedom and creativity.

The communication between the partners
redefines the roles of leader and follower. We
move to the floor only when both of us are ready.
I lead only where my partner is willing to follow,
and my partner anticipates and supports my lead.
We depend on each other, aware of how easily
we can look foolish from a false step. When we
become fluent in the same dance language, simul-
taneous shuffling becomes delightful art.

The transformation of a corporate culture
includes a transformation of its words, the learning
of a new dance of communication. Jesus Christ
was called the Word of God. He was God's way
of speaking the truth in love, inviting us to a new
dance with him.

ᔕTRENGTH

Your strength makes everything possible, God. Make me a strong leader.

God arms me with strength;
he has made my way safe.
Psalm 18:32

If the mission
really matters,
the only leader
worth following
is a strong leader.

A STRONG leader is the only kind of leader I want to follow, God, especially with purposes as important as ours. And it is the kind of leader I want to be. I don't want to be the boss; I want to be the leader.

I am not asking for the power to make people do what I want. I need some sort of authority, but I don't care if you give me formal, positional authority or informal, personal authority. I simply want to be the person who exercises decisive influence on the values and directions of the whole group, the one who holds them together and keeps them healthy and on task. I want to be the one they willingly go all the way with.

A weak leader is not really a leader at all, Lord. If you want me to lead, I have to be strong, and you will have to do it. I know you can. Nothing is impossible for you. I just do not know if you will. So I am saying to you plainly that if you grant a miracle of your strength in me and a miracle of your protection on my efforts and on the people I want to serve, then I can be the strong leader we need. Otherwise I cannot be the leader at all because we do not need a weak leader.

We need a leader with great influence, someone almost everyone trusts, someone who can enable us to get the job done. Only your strength can do this in me, and only your grace can move them to accept me as the leader. If you want someone else to lead, show me and everyone else that I am not the leader.

I am willing to lead with your strength, Lord. I think you have prepared me to lead. I have learned to follow well, so people can trust me to lead with a follower's heart. Help those I lead to be strong and active with me in the leadership process, not passive and simply compliant.

When I step out in leadership actions, either I will be persuasive and effective or I won't. If your strength can flow through me and make others feel strong when I lead, then you will have shown us again that . . .

Your strength makes everything possible, God. Make me a strong leader.

A WEAK LEADER IS NOT REALLY A LEADER AT ALL.

REFLECTIONS

Elder Toews was an ancient and venerated leader with enormous influence. I was the new administrator being brought in to turn things around. He took me to lunch to tell me two things:

1. From time to time a strong outsider is needed to bring necessary renewal. Neither I nor the renewal would be appreciated by the inner circle, so I would have to be strong and determined.
2. As long as I saw miracles happening, I could keep going. When I saw them ending, it would be time to step down.

In the years that followed, he returned to the same points with me often, encouraging me to press on and helping me understand the essence of strong leadership. He told me his own stories, which illustrated how leadership calls for voluntary sacrifice now in search of future excellence. Leadership enables people to risk the safe and comfortable present to gain a significantly different future.

He warned about weak leaders who suck strength out of their followers to keep themselves and the organization going, leaving the followers too weak to help lead. Strong leaders create energy in people, he said. They allow miracles to happen in the organization, helping the fearful to believe.

Shaking his bent finger at me, he made sure I understood that there is no such thing as a weak leader. Strong leadership is not a style or a set of behaviors. It is simply the only true leadership.

⌒ BUDGET

. . . .

*Everyone needs all your money
for right now, Lord. Help
us invest in our future.*

The budget declares
the operative values
and priorities of
the organization.
It also declares
our investment in
future directions.
The budget is a
leadership plan,
and budgeting is a
leadership process.

*Whoever sows sparingly
will also reap sparingly,
and whoever sows generously
will also reap generously.*
2 Corinthians 9:6, NIV

WE ARE your money managers, Lord. We are stewards, doing our best to make a budget that feeds and clothes your servants and that plants the money where you can use it best. We try to bring in as much money as we can and use it as shrewdly as we can. We never get it exactly right, but help us come close enough for an orderly operation and a good harvest.

The budget affects every person and every program, so getting it right is extremely important. Every budget line is someone's sincere request, wrapped in our mission and tied with their hopes. I love these people and pray for them. How I wish we could do it all for them! How many wonderful benefits have we needlessly killed because of our budgeting errors? I claim your forgiveness, Father. Teach me how to do it better this time.

God, somehow this budget has to give us both a present and a future. If I don't budget a strong present, I will have no platform to reach the future. If I don't manage well, I won't have anything to lead with. It is so hard to choose between what to do now and what to try later.

What powerful tyranny the urgencies of the present have! We must put the money where we say our true values are, but what is the right balance? After we care for all the current requirements, how will we pay for our future?

If we make a stingy investment in our future, we can expect a stingy harvest. Yet if the budget puts too much into preparing for our future, we will starve our chances for excellence now. Everything we plant for the future is something we cannot eat to be healthy right now. It is so hard to save for the future when we feel so poor. Somehow, by your grace, we must. Oh, Lord, give us wisdom and courage!

I know you have a bright future for us, but we will miss some of it if this budget does not help take us where you want us. Help me shape this budget into a wise leadership plan for an exciting future.

IT IS SO HARD TO CHOOSE BETWEEN WHAT TO DO NOW AND WHAT TO TRY LATER.

Everyone needs all your money for right now, Lord. Help us invest in our future.

REFLECTIONS

At the weddings of my two children, it was with great vested interest that I witnessed the solemn promises the young lovers made to each other. For people who are newly in love, such promises feel like they will be easy to keep, but every marriage eventually faces challenges to those commitments.

The core values of an organization are the promises its members make to each other. The budget is the most comprehensive and detailed description of what the organization has promised to do in expressing those values. What makes budgeting so difficult for a future-oriented leader is that the budget is mostly about history, about keeping promises that have already been made. If the promises were made wisely, they will have created a good set of present opportunities, attracted great people, secured a strong position in the market with a positive image, and allowed for increasing net revenues.

The need for growth is a product of the fundamental paradox in each budget. Driven mostly by the promises of history, the budget must also make promises to secure a future. The most brilliant plans for the most glowing future mean nothing until the budget lets them happen. The budget—mundane and arcane—is the ultimate leadership forum. It deserves whatever leadership attention is required to make it serve all its purposes well, and it deserves continuous prayer.

∽INTEGRITY

God, you are absolutely who
you claim to be. Keep me
true to myself.

Integrity is being
what I claim to
be and doing what
I promise to do.
A great leader
must demonstrate
personal integrity.

The integrity of the upright
guides them.
Proverbs 11:3, NIV

YOU MADE me, and you know me better than I know myself. Make certain that my personal character is always consistent with the leadership role I must fill. I want my leadership role to make me a better person. Only you can do this in me.

You know how I want people to agree with me and believe in me. It is so easy for me to say what others want to hear instead of what I honestly feel or believe. It is so natural for me to commit before I am positive I can deliver because someone needs something and I want to give it. Oh, God, set your Spirit at the door of my mouth, and guard what I say. Keep me honest and realistic.

Lord, in our markets, image is everything. My own image as the leader is a highly visible part of our organizational image. So often I am all that people know about the organization, and they read the fine print of what they see in me. If I do not seem genuine to them, they will assume the organization is not genuine either. Protect me from even the slightest fault of acting out of character.

Lord, I am not the leader every moment, but I am myself every moment. Those I lead depend on my integrity. Do not let me ever embarrass them, not as their leader and not as the real me inside the leader role. Make them safe in their dependence on me.

Don't let the fame and visibility that go with this leadership role fool me into forgetting the difference between myself and my role. Don't let me make the blunder of needing to be a celebrity. But by your grace, God, I would really love to be a genuine hero. I long to make a great difference in people's lives. I want to walk away someday and know that together we did something special and that we all became better people in the process. You can give the celebrity to someone else who needs it, God. Show me what I have to do to be an invisible hero, and empower me to do it.

God, you are absolutely who you claim to be. Keep me true to myself.

IT IS EASY FOR ME TO SAY WHAT OTHERS WANT TO HEAR INSTEAD OF WHAT I HONESTLY FEEL OR BELIEVE.

REFLECTIONS

The university had just managed to get through a very tough financial year. As CEO I had asked everyone to share in the sacrifices required to balance the budget. Many expenditure cuts had been needed, including a six-month delay in staff salary increases, but we ended the year in the black.

The board wanted to reward my leadership. They knew that I was being recruited by other organizations and that the year ahead looked strong, so they decided to give me a significant compensation boost. I thanked them for the intent of their affirmation but urged them to reconsider.

I needed to demonstrate fidelity to the fairness values we had invoked for the whole organization, even when it would have been easy to hide behind the justifiable action of the board. Finding wisdom on the matter, the board offered me deferred income if future financial results supported it. The event passed without much notice.

Integrity means being what you claim to be and doing what you promise to do.

I found out years later that the faculty was indeed watching for integrity—of a CEO who would share the sacrifice and a board that would risk losing their CEO. During the planning process for the next year, broad discretion was granted to the administration and the board, the reward for simple integrity.

⌒COMPASSION

*Give me the courage to lead
with wise compassion.*

*Because of the Lord's
great love we are not
consumed, for his
compassions never fail.*
Lamentations 3:22, NIV

The leader seeks
a future of
excellence for the
whole organization,
compassion for each
individual member.

BECAUSE you love me so strongly, I want to become everything you had in mind when you made me. I want to become more and more like you. I want to excel in every aspect of maturity. I want to be the best possible leader, who helps everyone in the organization experience the thrill of making a key contribution to a great success. God, I know you want these same experiences for every one of us.

Because you love me so tenderly, I trust your consoling compassion for all my shortcomings, incapacities, and broken dreams. I feel secure with you even when I do not act as you want me to and when I fail to lead well or fail to lead at all. God, I know you want everyone in the organization to feel the same kind of security, but compassion has a high price in our competitive environment.

Lord, I am called to lead the whole organization forward, but I am also responsible for the welfare of each person along the way. The organization exists to help build great people by serving people's real needs with excellence. For so many of us to labor together and serve so many, we need fair policies that express your compassion.

Yet sometimes what seems wise policy for everyone in general also seems to hurt someone in particular. What is the proper compassion for the individual who cannot contribute what we really need in order to reach our goals? If someone is not carrying his fair share of the load, it damages and discourages the others. What is the proper compassion for the individual whom we did not serve well? If I make a compassionate exception for one employee or one customer, I can easily force an unfair hardship on others.

Lord, I cannot always discern the genuine problems that we should try to alleviate from the imagined or even fraudulent ones. I need your light to ensure that in attempting to show compassion we aren't simply being gullible.

Give me the right sense of compassion. I need keen judgment to balance the needs of each individual with the needs of the organization and those we exist to serve. Help me to remember that with

WHEN I AM
CALLED TO LEAD
PEOPLE, I AM
RESPONSIBLE
FOR THEIR
WELFARE.

you mercy always triumphs over judgment. You want us to become like you, but when we fall short, your banner over us is loving compassion. Help me to mirror that compassion, both in policies and in exceptions.

Give me the courage to lead with wise compassion.

REFLECTIONS

The most difficult expression of compassion is
to tell someone that he cannot reasonably be
expected to accomplish what the organization
needs and should be removed from his position.
I have had to deliver such messages to staff,
administrators, and boards in my own organization
and in others. It has never once been an easy form
of compassion, but it is one of the most critical.

In the process I have come to understand Jesus'
compassion as not mainly about letting people off
the hook but enabling them to see their situation
more accurately, especially their potential. Jesus
enabled the blind to see, the lame to walk, the
demon-possessed to live in freedom, and fright-
ened fishermen to lead a spiritual movement that
affects the whole world.

It can be just as compassionate to remove a
person from a job in which he cannot succeed as
it is to cure someone's blindness. Working where it
is impossible to succeed destroys the inner person.
But compassion also requires us to help people
with any aspect of the transition that they cannot
reasonably do for themselves.

In the end, requiring such changes also shows
compassion for the organization, whose success
depends on top performance in each position.
Such actions are done well only with the spiritual
wisdom and courage that come through prayer.

ANGER

*Give me your anger, God,
against what is evil,
not against myself
or the people I love
and serve.*

Anger provides
enormous energy.
Righteous anger
empowers leaders
to conquer evil.
Wrongful anger
turns leaders
against the persons
they love and serve.
Turned inward, it
can induce severe
depression.

*Don't sin by letting anger
gain control over you.*
Ephesians 4:26

YOU ARE slow to your anger, God. Mine too often and too easily erupts immediately when provocation hits, unleashing my sharp tongue or my vengeance. Sometimes it leaves slashing scars that never disappear from the souls of those I care about. Turned on myself, my anger leaves me depressed. I need your Spirit to keep it under control. Protect me from myself.

When my anger burns hot or explodes openly, make me sensitive to what is really happening. If I am just venting to relieve my own frustration and insecurity, help me deal with the underlying cause in me. Help me learn the heart habit of pausing to check with you when I feel anger rising.

Give me the motivating power of your righteous anger, and purge from me the petulant destruction of selfish anger or anger at myself. I want to express anger in a way that will motivate people to great accomplishment, not belittle them in order to make me feel better.

I have been yelled at, falsely accused, and demeaned. It made me feel less like you, God, and it discouraged me. I do not want to treat peo-ple that way. I want to build them up and inspire them. I want to remember that these people do not exist to absorb pain from me. I exist to absorb their pain for them and to help them be strong. Do not let my anger diminish them or me.

I do not want to deny or try to suppress my

own anger or anyone else's. By your grace, I want to know the anger, learn from it, and express it for good. I do not want to lose my temper and waste all that power. I want to focus the angry energy where it will accomplish something positive.

Lord, you know that anger will come sometimes, but I do not want to live or lead in anger. I want to live and lead in love. Some appropriate anger about people's pain will properly grow out of your love at work in me. I want to inspire others, and be motivated myself, by noble passion for what is true, pure, lovely, and excellent in life. But I do not want any anger at all that results from defense of my wounded ego. If my ego is that vulnerable, I should not be leading anyway.

I DO NOT WANT ANY ANGER AT ALL THAT RESULTS FROM DEFENSE OF MY WOUNDED EGO.

I invite your Spirit to show me how you see each event in my leadership. I want to see what you see and feel what you feel. If there is anger . . .

Give me *your* anger, God, against what is evil, not against myself or the people I love and serve.

REFLECTIONS

Every time anger explodes inside me, burning to
be unleashed on the hapless person I am facing, I
see myself ten years old, writhing on the ground,
pounding my fists in the grass, crying and screaming.
My team had just lost a game of pickup football,
and my anger was totally out of control. My dad
walked across the field to me and firmly repri-
manded me for losing my temper.

"You lose your temper sometimes," I impu-
dently shot back.

There was a pause of awful silence during which
I finally came to my childish senses and became
frozen in fear. Dad spoke in a measured tone. "We
are both wrong to waste our energy by losing our
tempers. I will work at controlling mine if you will
learn to control yours."

In relief I nodded my unspoken assent.

My dad was a passionate leader. Passion is
essential to great leadership, and anger is the ready
passion of those who care intensely and expect
much from themselves and others. Most leaders
experience a great deal of anger, their own and
others'. But releasing uncontrolled anger inevitably
turns a person into a fool.

My dad's anger was just as strong after that
event as before, but he increasingly demonstrated
to me and to others what it meant to use it rather
than lose it. We kept the covenant we made with
each other that afternoon.

BOARD

Grant your special grace to the board, oh, Lord. We are entirely at the mercy of what it decides.

God has given each of us the ability to do certain things well. If God has given you leadership ability, take the responsibility seriously.
Romans 12:6, 8

The board of the organization is not just the ultimate legal entity; it is also the ultimate means of God's grace and blessing on the organization.

PUT the right people on the board, God, and give them the knowledge, skill, and insight to guide the organization with wise policies. If they are not the right people to begin with or are not well-informed or set foolish policies, we will all look foolish—including them. If they understand our situation and set wise policies, we will shine with success.

Do not let them be weak and overly cautious or we will miss opportunities. Do not let them mandate impossible or conflicting priorities or I will not know how to lead with integrity and we will fail and waste precious resources. Give them your Spirit of wisdom and courage so that we may achieve our mission with distinction.

Do not let them act as separate individuals, each with a personal agenda of issues or a particular constituency to represent, or the organization will end up a fractured reflection of their political compromises. Grant the board your Spirit of unity, with a strong and sincere consensus regarding the long-term good of the whole organization so that together we will reflect unity and cohesiveness.

Let them evaluate me based on specific desired outcomes and available resources that they have identified so I will know what direction to lead and we can all give our very best effort together. Spare us from micromanagement. Instill in the board a commitment to trust us for the outcomes they specify and to empower us to make our own way to excellence.

Let the board believe in us so we will be able to believe in ourselves. Let the board celebrate often in your Spirit of confidence.

If the board moves me into some leadership role, then I trust you for the grace to lead well. I also trust everyone in the organization to participate actively in the leadership process as we move forward together. If the board calls me to do more following, I will accept that as your wise and loving guidance for me and the organization. Show the board the person who should lead us.

LET THE BOARD BELIEVE IN US SO WE WILL BE ABLE TO BELIEVE IN OURSELVES.

Grant your special grace to the board, oh, Lord. We are entirely at the mercy of what it decides.

REFLECTIONS

She was a jewel: well educated, experienced, recommended to us by her church and ethnic community because of their great respect for her. I was trying to convince her to join the board of trustees. She supported the mission and vision of the university, but she saw no reason to join the board. She had spent her life supporting her husband, a well-known physician, raising successful children, and serving her church and community. Her one stint on the local school board had involved a highly public leadership crisis in which her integrity had prevented her reelection. We needed her, but she did not need us.

She was about to leave when I summarized my presentation with the simple explanation that the board was the spiritual mind and heart of the university and that what we really needed was her unique mind and heart that God had been shaping all these years through all the challenges she had met and mastered. We just needed who she was. For the first time, I saw the fire glimmer in her eyes.

"Mary," I said, "the board is so important that I pray for the trustees every single day. I will pray for you."

She left to ponder and in time became a wise and effective trustee. The organization can be no better than its board, and the board must be the focus of a leader's prayers.

⌒INTUITION

*Guide my hunch, God.
It needs to be a holy hunch.
It needs to be right.*

Strong leaders
create their own
vision, live by
their own standards,
and follow the
insight, foresight,
and wisdom of their
own intuition. They
also stay accountable
for what is truly
good for the people
affected by their
actions.

*The Lord will give you
insight into all this.*
2 Timothy 2:7, NIV

I WISH I could explain it all logically or factually for everyone, God. This one I just know somehow, without all the normal rational processes. I sense directly what the data mean, without all the steps. I see the beginning and the end without the middle. I feel it in my gut, and I think it is right, but the part of me that loves data and logic always complains. So will all the logical people around me, God, and who can blame them?

This is not the strong, nagging, uneasy type of hunch. This is a positive sense about what will really work, the confident feeling I get about certain people or proposals. This is one I want to try. But you know I cannot do this alone, God. Those I lead have to go with me, and there is no way to build the normal rationale. It is tough expecting people to risk themselves for my intuition.

It is almost always easier to stall things when I feel uneasy. There are always people who want to wait. It is harder to get people to move ahead when an airtight case has not been made either way. But if we wait too long to make a decision, it will be too late. Oh, Lord, why do we fear the risks of moving on so much more than the risks of sitting still?

If my hunches were right every time, this particular one would be easier. I am usually right when these intuitions are strong and focused, but I have been wrong a few times. So even more than usual, I am here to pause and listen to you. I do not want to run ahead of you, and I do not want to lag behind. I am grateful for strong people to hold me accountable. I need you to inform the intuitions of others on this one, either for or against. If this has to be decided on an informed hunch, it would help tremendously if several of us "hunched" in the same direction.

We really need a winner on this one, Lord. Let me hear your quiet, inner voice. I need a dark, doubtful sense of uneasiness if this hunch is wrong, and I need your bright, confirming peace if it is right.

Guide my hunch, God. It needs to be a holy hunch. It needs to be right.

WHY DO WE FEAR THE RISKS OF MOVING ON SO MUCH MORE THAN THE RISKS OF SITTING STILL?

REFLECTIONS

Virtually all leaders report that they depend on hunches or intuition to some significant degree. But it's hard to pray about something we do not understand and cannot explain. Some think intuition is simply ultrahigh-speed analysis and reasoning resulting from excellent learning in many similar experiences. Others are convinced that it is a suprarational gift that many people have but that only a few develop to a high level of effectiveness.

A third view is that in order to consistently leap to the right conclusion, the leader must invoke the appropriate values. Thus, many intuitive decisions are driven more by a sense of the morally right thing to do than by reasoning with the objective data. When I can base a decision more on values than on data, I am able to lead with great confidence and persuasive force.

Whether by one of these means or by some combination, intuitive leaders can be so sure of themselves, so secure in the inner person, so often right, and so convincing that they inspire others to trust them and follow their leadership to great achievements. Intuitive leadership can slip into the dangerous extreme of blinding charisma. But the noblest of intuitive leaders combine an inner spiritual light with the *agape* love of a true servant and are willing to test their hunches with others in leadership prayer.

CREATIVITY

Send your Spirit of freedom,
and break me out.

Creativity is
hazardous, but
lack of creativity
is fatal. Effective
leaders encourage
creativity by
modeling it
personally and
by protecting
and rewarding
it in others.

Wherever the Spirit of the
Lord is, he gives freedom.
2 Corinthians 3:17

I HAVE trapped myself in a box that I can't even recognize, Lord. You are the one who sets prisoners free. Release me. I am ready to leave the box of my normal thinking, willing to destroy it in the process, if that is what it takes. I must find the opportunity that lies disguised in this problem. Show me the truth that will set me free.

I am a prisoner of my old ways of thinking. My assumptions blind me to new possibilities that you have for me. What I think I know keeps me from knowing what I cannot yet think. I see people's weaknesses; you see the strengths you gave them. I see what they have done so far; you see what they could do. I see why we can't do it; you see how we can. I see the limits of our visible resources; you see the potential of your unlimited resources. I see the problem; you see the solution. Break me out.

Do you need to move me to a new place for a different view? Am I protecting something or someone? Am I protecting myself? What am I afraid of in this situation? Have I surrounded myself with people who think too much alike? too much like me?

You created this universe from nothing, lacing all of its expanding and self-renewing intricacies together in absolute perfection. You anticipated that we humans would sin and separate ourselves from you and your creation, so you created the perfect solution for our hopeless mess in Jesus Christ. You are the Father of all creativity.

I am your child. You made me in your image, so I, too, love to create. I love to think new thoughts and bring them into existence. I love to create solutions for the messes people get into. I want to be creative like you, Father. I want to enjoy all kinds of people. Give me the creative freedom of your Spirit. Silence my censors, and awaken the slumbering artist within. Give me a new song to sing, a new story to write.

107

I LOVE TO THINK NEW THOUGHTS AND BRING THEM INTO EXISTENCE.

I tried to be creative, and I worked myself into this dungeon.

Send your Spirit of freedom, and break me out.

REFLECTIONS

Consistently successful organizations are constantly improving, constantly learning new ways to think and act, and are therefore just slightly out of control. A leader's most important contributions to such corporate creativity are to staff for strengths, to maintain a high tolerance for ambiguity, and to demonstrate personal creativity. Each is risky activity.

Creativity depends on bringing differences together. For creative decision teams, the leader must ensure that the organization proactively identifies and honors all the necessary types: those who are wise—and possibly cautious; brave—and possibly foolhardy; artistic—and possibly impractical; pessimistic—and possibly cynical; optimistic—and possibly gullible.

By requiring such wide diversity, we not only risk the serious flaws that often accompany great talent, but we also increase the potential for conflict. Innovative organizations are exciting, but they are not tranquil. They are productive and progressive, but they are not peaceful.

Contradiction is often a necessary element of a constantly self-reforming organization with its face to a future that may be inherently contradictory. The most difficult contradiction for many leaders occurs when the leader's own cherished idea or program must be questioned or altered. If the leader can initiate the necessary changes or support those who do, a compelling message is sent about the core value of creativity. The leader doesn't have to provide all the creativity—just inspire, protect, reward, and pray for it.

DISCOURAGEMENT

*Bring the renewal my spirit
needs to keep on leading.*

Disappointment,
discouragement, and
despair constantly
hunt the leader's
spirit. The leader's
inner self-renewal is
essential, but so are
external protection
and support from
others. No great
leader leads alone.

*No one is here to comfort me;
any who might encourage me
are far away.*
Lamentations 1:16

DISAPPOINTMENT and dissent are facts of leadership, and I expect them, God. Normally they don't take me down or make me doubt like this. But sometimes the restraints, resistance, and reversals feel so overwhelming that there is no clear path to the goal. I feel as if I have been pushing a rock uphill with a lot of people telling me I will never make it. Maybe they are right.

Things are going badly, and I am disappointed in myself. But I am not just disappointed, Lord, and not just tired. I am really discouraged. My body is strong enough, but my spirit is weak; my will is failing. If something doesn't improve soon, I will despair entirely and give up trying to make this happen at all. I am not sure this is worth it anymore, or maybe I am not the right person to lead it. I feel like I am all alone and no one else really cares enough to do anything.

What do all these foul feelings mean? Are you trying to tell me we should cut our losses and quit this effort, or are these just barriers that we have to get past? Maybe this was a stupid thing to even start. I need some kind of sign if you want me to keep going. Send something, or send someone. I've had it, Father. I can't keep going like this.

When others get discouraged, I feel it, just as they will start feeling it from me. Maybe that downward cycle has already started. I sense that they are disappointed with me as their leader. I haven't met their expectations or their needs, and we are floundering.

I know you forgive me and love me, and your Spirit comforts me, and I am deeply grateful. But I need you to send me a touch or a word of insight or encouragement in human form. I feel like no one else knows where I am in this. Worse, maybe they just don't care. If no one else cares, maybe I shouldn't care either.

It takes faith to quit and faith to keep on, so this is not about my faith in you, God. It is about confidence in myself and about whether to keep leading in this direction. If I am supposed to quit leading on this one, does that signal that I should quit leading altogether? I am at your mercy, Father. If you want me to press forward, send a messenger who will . . .

Bring the renewal my spirit needs to keep on leading.

I NEED SOME KIND OF SIGN IF YOU WANT ME TO KEEP GOING.

REFLECTIONS

During his years heading Youth for Christ in the U.S., Jay Kesler also preached forty Sundays a year in his home church. On one occasion he was asked about a certain situation in which people were acting in nasty and petty ways. "I am very disappointed with the church," he said, "but I am not discouraged." The distinction stuck with me. It was part of how he carried such enormous responsibilities with such a joyful heart, and how he turned his own mistakes into growth experiences for himself and all those around him. He admitted disappointment and often found humor in it, but he wisely guarded his heart against discouragement.

Disappointment is not fatal to leadership. It goes with the territory. Indeed, part of what qualifies a person to lead is the ability to cope positively with criticism, mistakes, and failures. Every leader shows some version of "thick skin" because disappointment is ubiquitous. If we cannot take the arrows of disappointment, we cannot lead.

But disappointment differs from discouragement or despair, when we must admit that further pursuit of the goal makes no sense, when a particular person can no longer be trusted, when support would be wasted, when pearls would be cast before swine. Unlike disappointment, discouragement cannot be managed safely in isolation. The discouraged leader needs the touch of trusted and loving friends who bring the healing consolation of prayer.

⌒ CHANGE

Oh, Lord, give me faith for this leap to the future. And make this a leap of leadership, not a solo jump.

Leadership is inherently about effecting change in order to obtain some desired future condition that would not otherwise happen. Most people want progress as long as they do not have to change very much to get it.

No one puts new wine into old wineskins.
Luke 5:37

WHY CAN'T you give me a bridge to the future, Lord? Instead, you make me jump for it. You make me let go and leap by faith. You did it when I wanted a new relationship with you. You have done it repeatedly in my career and in my personal life. The new future you show me is beautiful, and the jump is reasonable, but it is always a leap of faith. So here I am again, asking for faith to make another leap.

This is a leadership leap, God. It will do no good if I make it and no one else even tries. I am not leading unless someone is following. Is anyone else going to leap with me? I am depending on you to spread this faith to others.

Is this change even possible? I need to feel sure I have not missed a fatal indicator. There is a fine line between faith and folly. Maybe we can't leap this far; two leaps won't work across a gap. Protect me from leading us off the edge. Confirm that we can make it.

Getting to this new future will change things for all of us. I cannot foresee all the changes, but I know there will be outcomes we did not intend. Don't let people worry unnecessarily about the unknowns, for if they hold back too much, we will not succeed.

You put us where we are, and it is so good and

comfortable. How you got us to this place is part of our tradition. Where we need to go looks uncertain, and it feels scary and even wrong in a way to lose and destroy what you have provided. Give us pilgrim's hearts, God. Do not let us clutch the present comfort and safety because it will not stay that way forever. We must leave this good place and move on, by faith—the same kind of faith that got us here.

If this change is going to happen, I need the right words from you—words to reduce anxiety, increase confidence, and intensify the feeling that we need to do it. Give me words that will show respect for our past as we head for our future together. But above all . . .

Oh, Lord, give me faith for this leap to the future. And make this a leadership leap, not a solo jump.

THERE IS A
FINE LINE
BETWEEN FAITH
AND FOLLY.

REFLECTIONS

In the guest bathroom of a friend's home, I found
no reading material, only a Rubik's Cube. Pondering
the challenges of leadership while fiddling with the
plastic puzzle, I happened upon these lessons:

Some Things Cannot Be Changed.
The center square determines what color each
side of the cube must be. Everything else about the
cube can be changed in endless permutations, but
the color of any one face is determined by the center. Inherently optimistic, I assume I can accomplish
whatever the organization needs, but I have always
been blessed with a few faithful "reality therapists"
who make sure we do not waste time and energy
trying to do the impossible.

You Can Never Change Just One Thing.
The only way to move any square on any face
of the cube is to move twelve squares all at once.
I may want to move one manager, rewrite one
section of the plan, modify one advertising concept,
drop one product line, add one new customer
service, or relocate one branch office. But every
change has multiple results, planned and otherwise.

*You Have to Give Up What You
Have to Get What You Want.*
Getting one face of the cube all the same color is
not too difficult, but progress beyond that point
requires losing part of that beautifully complete
face. Most people fail the cube because they cannot
destroy the first complete face they achieve. They
cling to the lovely but unfinished present and sacrifice the future.

LOVE

Give me your love for these people.
Love them through me.

Let us continue to love one another, for love comes from God.
1 John 4:7

No one should support or follow a leader who does not truly love him. No one should attempt to lead people he does not care about.

HOW I have come to love these people, God! I care about them with an extraordinary love that is far beyond myself. I do not profess to understand the passion I feel for their welfare, their development, their success, their reputation. What a priceless treasure you have given me—this joy, this privilege of loving them like this. It overflows in me and gilds my whole life.

Strange, in a way, to love them like this, because they can drive me crazy. I suffer with all their faults every day, magnified by the pressures of the performance standards and corporate goals we all agreed to. They question me, challenge me, ignore me, and resist me. They act like children when I do not ask their advice, and like infants if I do not follow it.

Yet see how gloriously they shine! How amazing they are, expertly accomplishing the special purposes that their unique talents and spiritual gifts enable them to fulfill. How smoothly they coordinate their labor. What marvels of creativity they fashion each day. See the deft skills they apply to meet real human needs. And see how they push themselves to grow, to be ever better. How beautifully they serve the noble calling of your kingdom. Magnificent, God, absolutely magnificent!

You showed them to me. You taught me how

to see who they really are, to see them as you do. And whenever I see them your way, your love always overwhelms me and pours out toward them. To open my eyes, you first love me. And as I feel your Spirit loving me, I can't help wanting whatever makes them more like you.

I love them for making me their leader. They have blessed me with their trust after I was wrong and with their encouragement when I was weary. They have carried me when I was injured and taught me what I needed to know in order to lead them well. They have respected me and forgiven my failures. They have protected my reputation and called me their friend. They have loved me.

I love them. But just my love would never be enough. They need and deserve much more. With all my heart and strength I pray . . .

Give me your love for these people. Love them through me.

I CARE ABOUT
THESE PEOPLE
WITH AN
EXTRAORDINARY
LOVE THAT IS
FAR BEYOND
MYSELF.

REFLECTIONS

I have led, and I have followed, and in both roles I have loved and been loved. First Corinthians 13:13 says, "There are three things that will endure—faith, hope, and love—and the greatest of these is love." One of the truths I have come to see in light of this verse is that love, having once been expressed, never completely goes away. Love changes us permanently because we become new people from living the adventure together.

The other truth of this verse that informs leadership is that loving people is eternal. In heaven we will no longer need faith or hope. We will experience fully what on earth we only believed in and hoped for. But in heaven we will go on loving and being loved. Love remains forever.

I have concluded, therefore, that leadership and followership are both about loving people, as they are and as they could be. But even more, the people who have followed my leadership have taught me that the essence of leadership is taking the risk of letting myself be loved however the followers choose to love me. It takes spiritual courage to experience leadership love this way, but by God's grace, through sincere prayer, it is possible.